This Log Book belongs to

____

If found please phone

____

Date

Location

GPS

Machine used

Machine settings

Items Found

Notes

Date

Location

GPS

Machine used

Machine settings

Items Found

Notes

Date

Location

GPS

Machine used

Machine settings

Items Found

Notes

Date

Location

GPS

Machine used

Machine settings

Items Found

Notes

Date

Location

GPS

Machine used

Machine settings

Items Found

Notes

Date

Location

GPS

Machine used

Machine settings

Items Found

Notes

Date

Location

GPS

Machine used

Machine settings

Items Found

Notes

Date

Location

GPS

Machine used

Machine settings

Items Found

Notes

Date

Location

GPS

Machine used

Machine settings

Items Found

Notes

Date

Location

GPS

Machine used

Machine settings

Items Found

Notes

Date

Location

GPS

Machine used

Machine settings

Items Found

Notes

Date

Location

GPS

Machine used

Machine settings

Items Found

Notes

Date

Location

GPS

Machine used

Machine settings

Items Found

Notes

Date

Location

GPS

Machine used

Machine settings

Items Found

Notes

Date

Location

GPS

Machine used

Machine settings

Items Found

Notes

Date

Location

GPS

Machine used

Machine settings

Items Found

Notes

Date

Location

GPS

Machine used

Machine settings

Items Found

Notes

Date

Location

GPS

Machine used

Machine settings

Items Found

Notes

Date

Location

GPS

Machine used

Machine settings

Items Found

Notes

Date

Location

GPS

Machine used

Machine settings

Items Found

Notes

Date

Location

GPS

Machine used

Machine settings

Items Found

Notes

Date

Location

GPS

Machine used

Machine settings

Items Found

Notes

Date

Location

GPS

Machine used

Machine settings

Items Found

Notes

Date

Location

GPS

Machine used

Machine settings

Items Found

Notes

Date

Location

GPS

Machine used

Machine settings

Items Found

Notes

Date

Location

GPS

Machine used

Machine settings

Items Found

Notes

Date

Location

GPS

Machine used

Machine settings

Items Found

Notes

Date

Location

GPS

Machine used

Machine settings

Items Found

Notes

Date

Location

GPS

Machine used

Machine settings

Items Found

Notes

Date

Location

GPS

Machine used

Machine settings

Items Found

Notes

Date

Location

GPS

Machine used

Machine settings

Items Found

Notes

Date

Location

GPS

Machine used

Machine settings

Items Found

Notes

Date

Location

GPS

Machine used

Machine settings

Items Found

Notes

Date

Location

GPS

Machine used

Machine settings

Items Found

Notes

Date

Location

GPS

Machine used

Machine settings

Items Found

Notes

Date

Location

GPS

Machine used

Machine settings

Items Found

Notes

Date

Location

GPS

Machine used

Machine settings

Items Found

Notes

Date

Location

GPS

Machine used

Machine settings

Items Found

Notes

Date

Location

GPS

Machine used

Machine settings

Items Found

Notes

Date

Location

GPS

Machine used

Machine settings

Items Found

Notes

Date

Location

GPS

Machine used

Machine settings

Items Found

Notes

Date

Location

GPS

Machine used

Machine settings

Items Found

Notes

Date

Location

GPS

Machine used

Machine settings

Items Found

Notes

Date

Location

GPS

Machine used

Machine settings

Items Found

Notes

Date

Location

GPS

Machine used

Machine settings

Items Found

Notes

Date

Location

GPS

Machine used

Machine settings

Items Found

Notes

Date

Location

GPS

Machine used

Machine settings

Items Found

Notes

Date

Location

GPS

Machine used

Machine settings

Items Found

Notes

Date

Location

GPS

Machine used

Machine settings

Items Found

Notes

Date

Location

GPS

Machine used

Machine settings

Items Found

Notes

Printed in Great Britain
by Amazon

13753899R00059